MADAME CHIANG KAI-SHEK: FACE O
AUTHOR: Donovan, Sandra.
Reading Level: 8.2
Point Value: 2.0
Accelerated Reader Quiz # 107912

MADAME
CHIANG KAI-SHEK
FACE OF MODERN CHINA

SPECIAL LIVES IN HISTORY THAT BECOME

Signature LIVES

MADAME
CHIANG KAI-SHEK
FACE OF MODERN CHINA

by Sandy Donovan

Content Adviser: Kevin G. Cai, Ph.D.,
Assistant Professor, Department of Asia Pacific Studies,
San Diego State University

Reading Adviser: Susan Kesselring, M.A.,
Literacy Educator,
Rosemount–Apple Valley–Eagan
[Minnesota] School District

COMPASS POINT BOOKS  MINNEAPOLIS, MINNESOTA

Compass Point Books
3109 West 50th Street, #115
Minneapolis, MN 55410

Visit Compass Point Books on the Internet at *www.compasspointbooks.com*
or e-mail your request to *custserv@compasspointbooks.com*

Editor: Jennifer VanVoorst
Page Production: Noumenon Creative
Photo Researcher: Svetlana Zhurkin
Cartographer: XNR Productions, Inc.
Library Consultant: Kathleen Baxter

Art Director: Jaime Martens
Creative Director: Keith Griffin
Editorial Director: Carol Jones
Managing Editor: Catherine Neitge

Library of Congress Cataloging-in-Publication Data
Donovan, Sandra, 1967–
    Madame Chiang Kai-shek: face of modern China / by Sandy Donovan.
        p. cm. — (Signature lives)
        Includes bibliographical references and index.
    ISBN-13: 978-0-7565-1886-8 (hardcover)
    ISBN-10: 0-7565-1886-5 (hardcover)
    ISBN-13: 978-0-7565-1989-6 (paperback)
    ISBN-10: 0-7565-1989-6 (paperback)
        1. Chiang, May-ling Soong, 1897–   —Juvenile literature. 2. Presidents'
spouses—China—Biography—Juvenile literature. 3. Presidents' spouses—
Taiwan—Biography—Juvenile literature. I. Title. II. Title: Face of
    modern China. III. Series.
    DS777.488.C515D66 2007
    951.24'905092—dc22
        [B]   2006002999

MODERN WORLD

From 1900 to the present day, humanity and the world have undergone major changes. New political ideas resulted in worldwide wars. Fascism and communism divided some countries, and democracy brought others together. Drastic shifts in theories and practice tested the standards of personal freedoms and religious conventions as well as science, technology, and industry. These changes have created a need for world policies and an understanding of international relations. The new mind-set of the modern world includes a focus on humanitarianism and the belief that a global economy has made the world a more connected place.

Madame Chiang Kai-shek

Table of Contents

1 MAKING A CASE FOR CHINA

Chapter

❦

The members of the U.S. Congress were mostly quiet as the small, thin woman in traditional Chinese dress entered the Senate chamber. Once she had been escorted to a seat, she turned, and the senators and representatives, standing, burst into a round of applause. It was February 18, 1943—the height of World War II—and the wife of the generalissimo of the Chinese army would be the first Chinese person, and the second woman, to ever address a joint session of the U.S. House and Senate.

Madame Chiang Kai-shek spoke in perfect English with a trace of the Southern accent she had picked up as a high school student in Georgia. She told the U.S. Congress:

Madame Chiang Kai-shek, standing next to Senator Sam Rayburn, addressed Congress at the beginning of her U.S. tour.

Madame Chiang Kai-shek was the second woman to address a joint session of the U.S. Congress. Suffragist Victoria Woodhull was the first. In 1871, she addressed the U.S. House and Senate, arguing in favor of women's right to vote. The following year, she made history again by becoming the first woman to run for president of the United States.

The traditional friendship between your country and mine has a history of one hundred and sixty years. I feel ... that there are a great number of similarities between your people and mine and that the similarities are the basis for our friendship.

In fact, the United States and China did have much in common during those years of world conflict. Both nations were at war with the Japanese. The United States and Japan were on opposite sides in the World War II conflict, and the Chinese had been fighting Japanese invaders for nearly 10 years. But there were also many differences between the two countries. The United States was a representative democracy whose president, Franklin Delano Roosevelt, had worked tirelessly throughout the Great Depression to help poor Americans achieve success. Meanwhile, China was led by Generalissimo Chiang Kai-shek, a dictator who ruled with an iron fist, often executing enemies for little reason and ignoring the widespread disease and starvation of the Chinese people.

Although the U.S. government was aware of many of Chiang Kai-shek's faults, it also knew that it needed

China to help defeat the Japanese. So throughout the war, it had sent billions of dollars to China. Some of this money had bought new weapons for the Chinese army, and some had bought luxury items for the woman now standing in front of the Congress. None of it, however, had helped lift the Chinese people out of the poverty they endured.

That day, Madame Chiang Kai-shek had come to plead for more assistance and to convince the members of Congress that the future of China would affect the future of the United States. In her brief speech, she told Congress that the Chinese were being persecuted by the brutal Japanese army and that it was within America's power to improve the lives of millions of suffering Chinese. Most of all,

The United States sent soldiers, air-planes, and money to help China win its fight against Japan.

however, she wanted to put an Americanized face—hers—on China.

Madame Chiang Kai-shek was both smart and glamorous, and she made a lasting impression on those who met her. She told the the U.S. senators and representatives:

> *I came to your country as a little girl. I know your people. ... I speak your language, not only the language of your hearts, but also your tongue. ... I feel that if the Chinese people could speak to you in your own tongue, or if you could understand our tongue, they would tell you that basically and fundamentally, we are fighting for the same cause.*

Madame Chiang showed her true personality in her speech before Congress. She was charming and well-spoken, she flattered the audience, and she was a little bit false as well. She told the Congress that she had not expected to make a full speech to them and so was speaking from her heart. She said that her words were spur-of-the-moment, and she contrasted herself with politicians who made numerous drafts of each speech. In reality, however, Madame Chiang had carefully planned out her words. She knew that U.S. support was critical to the survival of her husband's government, and she was willing to work as hard as she could to gain that support.

She succeeded brilliantly in earning the support of the U.S. Congress. When she set out on a tour of the United States soon after her address, she also won the support—and the donations—of thousands of Americans. Before heading back to China, she stayed with President Roosevelt at the White House and dined with movie stars in Hollywood.

This tour of the United States was probably the finest moment in the life of this privileged and powerful woman. Born into a wealthy Chinese family, Madame Chiang desired power all her life and imagined that, with her husband, she would one day be a respected world leader like President Roosevelt. But within six years of her American success, the Chiangs were forced out of mainland China. Though they would spend the rest of their lives in exile, the mark they made on history was so great that Madame Chiang Kai-shek is still remembered as the face of modern China and one of the most powerful women of the 20th century. 🙠

Madame Chiang Kai-shek (1898–2003)

2 A MODERN GIRL

❦

Madame Chiang Kai-shek was born Soong Meiling in 1898 in Shanghai, China. She was the fourth of six children in the well-known and powerful Soong family. Her father, Charlie Soong, was a successful businessman—one of the wealthiest in China. He was also one of the few Christians in China at that time.

Charlie Soong was born Soong Yao-ju on the southern Chinese island of Hainan. At the age of 9, he left the island by stowing away inside a large ship. Three years later, he arrived in the United States and was taken in by a family in North Carolina. The family raised him as a Christian and sent him to Vanderbilt University in Nashville, Tennessee. Yao-ju took the name of Charles Jones, after a famous sea captain. At Vanderbilt, he earned a certificate in theology—the

By 1910, 12-year-old Soong Meiling had been living in the United States for two years.

study of religion—and then moved back to Shanghai in 1886. The family in North Carolina hoped he would act as a Christian missionary and spread the word of Jesus in China. Charlie Soong was more interested in making a fortune than in spreading Christianity, but he found a way to do both. He started a successful business printing Bibles.

Soong married a religious Christian, Ni Kwei-tseng, from a very old Chinese family. His printing business soon made him very wealthy, and the family had six children. When their daughter Meiling was born in 1898, she had two older sisters and a brother. Her sisters Ailing and Qingling were 8 and 6, and her brother Tse-ven was 4. By then, the Soongs were the wealthiest family in Shanghai. This city had once been one of China's grandest cities, but at this time it was just a village with muddy banks along the Whangpoo River, about 17 miles (27 kilometers) from the mighty Yangtze River. The young Soongs were known throughout the city as the children of "Charlie" and "Mammy," which was the nickname

The Soong family is remembered today as one of the most influential Chinese families of the early 1900s. Although there were six children, it is the three daughters who are most remembered. A common saying is that of the three Soong daughters, one loved money (Ailing, who married one of the world's richest bankers, H.H. Kung); one loved power (Meiling, who married Chiang Kai-shek); and one loved China (Qingling, who married Sun Yat-sen and later sided with the Chinese Communists).

Shanghai has a long history as one of the most important cities in China.

everybody used for Meiling's mother. As Christians, and with a father who was educated in the United States, the Soongs were a modern family. Ailing is still remembered as the first Chinese girl to ride a bicycle in Shanghai.

At 8 years old, Meiling began attending the

Motyeire School, a private American school in Shanghai. Education was important in the Soong family, and Meiling worshipped both of her parents. She admired her father and knew that everyone in Shanghai greatly respected him. But she was most impressed by her mother's devotion to God. Mammy spent hours each day praying, often getting up before dawn to begin. Meiling later remembered, "As long as my mother lived, I had a feeling that whatever we did, or failed to do, she would pray me through."

At the time, China was ruled by an emperor, but many Chinese people thought the emperor was unfair and were working to overthrow him. Sun Yat-sen led a group called the Kuomintang, or Nationalists, that wanted to create a new, modern China.

Sun Yat-sen
(1866–1925)

The Soongs were not particularly involved with politics, but they understood that China was going to change greatly in the years to come, and they wanted to make sure their children were prepared. All of the Soong children were sent to the United States for school. Charlie and Mammy wanted their children to receive a Christian education to be prepared for life in modern China. But most importantly, they knew that dangerous times were coming in China, and they wanted their children to be safely far away.

So in 1908, at the age of 10, Meiling traveled to Macon, Georgia. She lived near the campus of Wesleyan College for Women, where her older sister Ailing was already a student. Meiling did not attend the college, but Wesleyan students tutored her in English and other subjects. She learned the new language quickly and spoke it with a Georgia accent.

Meanwhile, back in Shanghai, Meiling's father was secretly printing pamphlets for Nationalist leader Sun Yat-sen. With Soong's help, the Nationalists overthrew the emperor in late 1911, and Sun became the first president of the Republic of China the following year. Soong was now powerful both because of his wealth and because of his connection to Sun Yat-sen. But President Sun was soon forced out of office and fled to Japan. He hired Meiling's older sister Qingling

A doctor who had studied medicine in Hawaii, Sun Yat-sen led his first revolt against the Qing Dynasty in 1895. In 1912, after the overthrow of the emperor, he briefly became president of China. Sun created the Kuomintang, or Nationalist, political party, which was later led by Chiang Kai-shek. Sun dreamed of uniting all of China, at the time ruled by individual warlords, and declared the "Three People's Principles" of nationalism, democracy, and social reform. After his death in 1925, he became the patron saint of the Nationalist Party.

to be his secretary. Although Sun was 50 years old and Qingling was only 23, the couple married in 1915. Now the Soong family was directly connected to the Nationalist movement.

At the time of Qingling's marriage to Sun, Meiling was a college student, having left Georgia in 1913 to attend a well-known women's college, Wellesley College, near Boston, Massachusetts. Her older brother, Tse-ven, called T.V., lived nearby and studied at Harvard University. At Wellesley, Meiling lived with a family for her first year. She made friends right away because she loved to meet new people. She blended in with the American students because she dressed in the latest styles, but her Chinese looks made her seem more glamorous. By now her English was nearly perfect, but her Georgia accent was unusual in the northern state of Massachusetts.

At the beginning of her second year at Wellesley, Meiling moved into a dormitory on the Wellesley campus. She studied English literature and philosophy.

She continued to make friends easily. During her four years at Wellesley, she joined an art and music society, swam, and played tennis. Her college friends remembered her as outgoing and popular, and according to one friend, "There always seemed to be some nice Chinese boy or other on the doorstep."

Wellesley College was founded in 1870 to provide women with educational opportunities equal to those of men.

Meiling graduated from Wellesley College with a degree in English literature.

In 1917, Meiling graduated with honors from Wellesley and returned to China. She later said that the only thing Oriental, or Asian, about her was her face.

After having lived 11 years in the United States, Meiling felt more American than Chinese. China and the United States are located on opposite sides of the globe, and in the early 1900s, the differences between them were great. Ever since the Industrial Revolution, life in the United States had become more and more modern as cars, electric lights, and telephones became common. Following success in World War I, the United States was also entering a period of great wealth and excitement. Americans generally felt positive about themselves and their country. Meanwhile, China was less modernized, and many people were living in poverty. The country was still in the middle of a violent revolution following the overthrow of the last emperor.

Differences between the lives of Chinese women and American women were particularly strong. In the United States, more and more women were becoming independent, entering the workforce, and demanding the same rights as men. The suffrage movement ended with the passage of the 19th Amendment in 1920, giving American women the right to vote. In China during this period, however, women still lived as they had for centuries. Very few were educated as Meiling was, and even fewer held jobs outside the home. Hardly any Chinese women were interested in politics.

When Meiling returned to Shanghai in 1917, she had spent almost as much of her life in the United States as in China, and she had grown to love the culture and people of her adopted country.

> *Although in the early 1900s the conditions of women in China lagged behind those of their U.S. counterparts, some Chinese women were actively working to improve their circumstances and advance their rights. The Chinese Suffragette Society demanded political and voting rights for women and an end to the traditional practice of foot binding (in which girls' feet were broken and bound to make them very small). Chinese women eventually gained the right to vote in 1949.*

Now, Shanghai seemed new and strange, but Meiling was happy to be home. She was also determined to bring some of the best of the United States to her own country. She knew it would be hard for the Chinese to accept many American ideas and values. And she knew that to get the Chinese people to understand what the United States had to offer, she would have to first understand Chinese people.

Meiling got to work improving her Chinese and studying traditional Chinese literature and culture. She also studied traditional Chinese painting under two great masters of the art. Soon she began doing social work for the Young Women's Christian Association (YWCA) in Shanghai. This Christian social organization worked to spread Christian values in China. Meiling became known in Shanghai for her work with this group. She was especially interested in encouraging young Chinese women to get an education.

In the early 1900s, Chinese children were often educated in unconventional places, such as a school run by a railway signal operator by the side of a railway track.

Soon Meiling was asked to be a member of Shanghai's Child Labor Commission. As a member of that group, she studied the way children worked in China. Many young children were sent to work on farms and in factories. The work was hard, and they earned very little money. But their families needed whatever money the children could earn to help buy food. Meiling thought Chinese children—both boys and girls—should go to school like American children, and she spoke about her beliefs to many of the powerful leaders who were friends with her father. People in Shanghai respected Meiling, but many thought she was too Americanized. ✍

3 BECOMING MADAME CHIANG

Chapter

꒰⚬×⚬꒱

In 1922, when Meiling was 24 years old and living with her parents in Shanghai, she was introduced to Chiang Kai-shek. Chiang was 11 years older than Meiling, and he was a rising star in the Chinese army. He was originally from southern China, where he had married very young in an arranged marriage. He had a son, Chiang Ching-kuo, with his first wife, but he left his family to follow his military career. By the 1920s, he had moved to Shanghai and married a second wife, Jennie. It was not uncommon in China at that time for men to be married to more than one woman.

Chiang worked as an aide to Sun Yat-sen, the Nationalist leader who was married to Meiling's sister Qingling. He was respected by Sun and other

On December 1, 1927, Chiang Kai-shek and Soong Meiling married in one of the grandest ceremonies of the time.

Nationalists because he followed their orders exactly. He was named the head of China's largest school for army officers. But Chiang had a much higher goal than being Sun's aide: He wanted to be the next leader of the Chinese Nationalists.

Chiang knew that being linked to the powerful Soong family would help him reach his goal. So when Soong Ailing invited Chiang and his wife Jennie to a dinner party in 1922, he was excited. "I want the

Chiang Kai-shek (standing), head of the Whampoa Military Academy, posed with the president of the Republic of China, Sun Yat-sen.

names of Sun, Soong and Chiang to be linked tightly together," he told his wife. Jennie remembered the dinner years later. Ailing and Meiling were both there, and Jennie said they "looked like they had stepped out of a Shanghai fashion book." Jennie noticed the two Soong sisters watching her husband all night, and she saw her husband watching them, too. At one point, she walked in a room and overheard the sisters talking about her. Ailing described her as "nothing more than a middle-class housewife" and asked, "How can she ever qualify to be the wife of a budding leader? Something must be done about it."

Jennie knew that both Chiang and the Soongs wanted to form a connection. Chiang wanted the power that the Soongs' money and connections could bring him, and the Soongs wanted the political power that they thought Chiang would soon have. In fact, Chiang's desire to be a part of the Soong family was so strong that after Sun Yat-sen died in 1925, he asked Qingling, Sun's widow and Meiling's sister, to marry him. Qingling refused his proposal. She later told people that she had always hated Chiang and that she thought the proposal was "politics, not love."

After Sun's death, several of his followers, including Chiang, were struggling to become the next Nationalist leader. Most of the country was ruled by violent warlords who fought bloody battles against each other. Whoever was going to lead China would first have to control these warlords. Two main political groups were fighting for control of China: the Nationalists and the Communists. Both groups wanted to end the great poverty in China. They both believed in a strong central government that would control most of the country's land and factories. But the Nationalists believed in traditional Chinese religion, culture, and values. The Communists did not believe in religion. They wanted to remake China to be like the powerful communist nation to its north, the Union of Soviet Socialist Republics (U.S.S.R.), or the Soviet Union. Chinese Communists wanted to fight against Chiang's Nationalist army, but the powerful Soviet leader Joseph Stalin ordered all Communists to support Chiang over the Chinese Communists.

As the head of the Nationalist army, Chiang set out to take over the northern Chinese cities of Hankou, Shanghai, and Nanking. To do this, he cooperated with the Chinese Communists and accepted money and supplies from the Soviet Union. But once he had conquered these cities, Chiang showed a violent side that surprised even Stalin, who was well-known for his own unfair attacks on innocent people. Chiang ordered the killing of anyone in Shanghai who seemed to side with the Communists. The event was called the Shanghai Massacre, and by the time it was over, Chiang's army had executed more than 5,000 Chinese citizens.

Chiang Kai-shek led a military patrol through southern China in 1925.

Many could not believe that Chiang could act so brutally toward his own fellow Chinese. Qingling, Sun Yat-sen's widow and Meiling's sister, called for Chiang to be thrown out of China. Meiling's brother, T.V., gave up his position as Nationalist finance minister because he didn't agree with Chiang's action. But Chiang was able to hang onto and even increase his power. Across China, as people heard about the killings, they became fearful of upsetting Chiang or of appearing to be against him.

At the beginning of Chiang's campaign to conquer China, Meiling had sent him a letter congratulating him on his early victories. Now, while her brother and sister were turning against Chiang, Meiling remained friendly with him. Chiang was becoming more interested in Meiling as well. People said that he had loved her since first meeting her three years earlier. Others said that he simply wanted to seal his connection with the Soongs. In any event, in 1927, Chiang asked Meiling to marry him. But Meiling said she would not marry him without her mother's consent. And Meiling's mother did not like Chiang for two reasons: First, he was already married; and second, he was not a Christian. But Chiang eventually convinced Meiling's mother to allow the marriage. He first sent Jennie away to the United States, telling the Soongs that he had divorced her. And he promised to soon become a Christian,

Chiang Kai-shek (1887–1975)

although he told his future mother-in-law that he couldn't become a Christian right away, because religion needed to be taken gradually, not swallowed like a pill.

Meiling eventually gained the approval of her family, and she and Chiang were married on December 1, 1927. Meiling was 29, and the groom was 40 years old. The wedding, like the marriage, combined the modern with the traditional and military might with social standing. First, a small Christian wedding was held at the Soongs' Shanghai mansion. A large military ceremony followed at Shanghai's grandest hotel, the Majestic Hotel. More than 1,300 guests attended, and a crowd of 1,000 gathered outside the hotel. The *Shanghai Times* called the wedding "the outstanding Chinese marriage ceremony of recent years." The bride wore a fitted silver and white gown and a 1920s flapper-style lace veil with flowers dripping off of it. She wore silver shoes and stockings and carried

After her marriage, Soong Meiling chose to be known as Madame Chiang to highlight that she was the wife of a leader. But in China, wives traditionally do not take their husbands' family names after marriage, as they do in many Western cultures. A Chinese person's first name is his or her family name, and the second name is the equivalent of a first name in Western cultures. Children use their father's family name.

a bouquet of pink roses. The groom wore a Western-style tuxedo jacket and striped pants. A Russian orchestra played Mendelssohn's "Wedding March." While newspaper cameras flashed, the couple faced each other beneath a large portrait of Sun Yat-sen and bowed three times. Soong Meiling was now Madame Chiang Kai-shek.

4 POWER COUPLE

❦

Although many observers believed that the Chiang marriage was a power union and not a love match, the Chiangs insisted that they were living a love story. Chiang spoke no English, but his wife taught him to call her "Darling." He once wrote to her:

> *Thinking about the people I admire in this life, you, my lady, are the only one. ... Recalling the hundreds of battles fought on the front and my own type of heroism, I cannot but feel that so-called achievement is just an illusion or a dream. And yet, my lady, your talent, beauty, and virtue are not things I can ever forget.*

At the time, most women did not take part in politics. But from the beginning of their marriage,

With their marriage, the Chiangs brought together the family influence of the Soongs and the political and military power of the Nationalists.

the Chiangs were partners. Madame Chiang traveled with her husband. She advised him and helped him make important military decisions. People who knew Chiang knew that he listened to his wife's advice.

One reason that Madame Chiang had power was that she spoke English so well. At the time, some American and English government leaders were living in Shanghai. It was important for the Nationalists to have these leaders on their side. But Chiang did not speak their language, and so Madame Chiang became her husband's interpreter. She told him what the American and English leaders

Chinese women often cared for the estates of wealthy foreign diplomats living in Shanghai, sometimes even weeding their lawns by hand.

were saying, and she repeated her husband's replies back to them. Often, she was the only person in a room who spoke both Chinese and English. This gave her great power over her husband and others. She could slightly change the meaning of the words she was interpreting. Sometimes she would tell her husband only what she wanted him to hear.

Early in their marriage, Madame Chiang began preparing daily news reports for her husband. She read all of the newspapers available in English. Then she translated the news of the day into Chinese for her husband. He often began his day in their mansion by reading over her news reports. Again, this allowed Madame Chiang to influence the news that her husband heard.

Apart from her English-language skills, Madame Chiang had other skills that greatly helped her husband. She understood American habits and customs better than most Chinese. She knew that some things that seemed normal to Chinese people might anger Americans. And she knew that some American customs that appeared rude to most

>
> *Most people in China speak a language called Mandarin. The spoken language has many versions, called dialects, that vary throughout the country, but it is always written the same way. Written Mandarin Chinese is made up of as many as 50,000 letters that are written as tiny pictures. Today, approximately one-fifth of the people in the world speak some form of Chinese as a native language.*

Chinese people were actually meant to be polite. For instance, Chinese people were not used to being asked personal questions by strangers, and they might find visitors who asked about their family or other personal matters rude. So she was able to interpret more than just words for her husband. She was able to let him know how the American and English leaders really felt about them. Perhaps most importantly, she was able to flatter and show respect to the Americans. This helped them to see the Nationalists in a good light.

As violent civil war between the Communists and the Nationalists continued, most people in China were living in poverty. More than 95 percent of the country's 450 million citizens lived in towns or villages with fewer than 100,000 residents. Most Chinese lived in villages with fewer than 20 homes, each built of mud and housing peasants and their animals together. There was no power, running water, or paved roads. There were fewer than 7,000 doctors and nurses, and almost no hospitals in the whole country. Most of the peasants could not read at all, and there were fewer than 1,000 high schools in all of China. Most of those, of course, were in the larger cities near the coasts.

In the city of Shanghai, the Chiangs lived very differently. The Nationalists controlled the city, and the pair was mostly treated like a king and queen.

Shanghai's many poor lived in crowded and often dirty conditions.

There was another group, however, that had just as much power. This was a group of gangsters called the Green Gang, led by a man nicknamed "Big-Eared Du."

The Green Gang ruled the city of Shanghai through fear, and in many ways they had more power than the Nationalists. They controlled most of the city's finances and banking, and they ran a large drug-smuggling ring. Big-Eared Du and his men made all of Shanghai's business and government leaders pay them "protection money." This money

By the late 1920s, the city of Shanghai was thriving once again, with a busy and modern downtown.

protected them from being attacked or even killed by Green Gang members. If Big-Eared Du asked a store owner to give him a large sum of money, the store owner would usually do so right away. If he did not hand over the requested money, he knew he risked being attacked. Sometimes the Green Gang gangsters beat their victims with sticks. That was usually all it took to convince someone to pay their protection money. But if they still didn't pay, Green Gang members would return to do something worse. They were not afraid to kill people who didn't pay them.

Since taking power in Shanghai, Chiang and the Nationalists had paid the Green Gang regularly. They did this so the gangsters would leave them alone. But when Madame Chiang discovered that her husband was paying protection money to the gangsters, she was angry. She told Chiang that as the leader of the Nationalists, he did not have to pay any gangsters. She told him that he should have the gangsters killed if they demanded money from him. Chiang did not think it would be that easy to get the Green Gang to leave him alone, but he agreed to try. He soon found out what a bad idea that was.

One day Madame Chiang went out to shop in

In the 1920s, the coastal city of Shanghai earned the nickname "Sin City" because of the many gambling houses and bars found throughout the city. Everyone was aware that the city's true boss was Big-Eared Du, head of the Green Gang gangsters. He controlled most of the vice in the city, including gambling, alcohol, and other drugs. Du worked closely with Chiang while Chiang was headquartered in Shanghai. He helped carry out the Shanghai Massacre, in which more than 5,000 suspected Communists were killed.

Shanghai's wealthy shopping area. As usual, she was driven in a fancy limousine by a uniformed driver. By that evening she had not returned home to the Chiangs' mansion. Chiang was worried about her. He knew that people who disobeyed Big-Eared Du

At the time she was kidnapped, Madame Chiang was living in luxury in Shanghai.

often disappeared. He also knew that those people might be found dead a day or two later. So Chiang telephoned Big-Eared Du, who told Chiang that his wife was fine and was, in fact, at Du's office. It wasn't a very wise thing for a woman to be out alone, Du said. When his men found Madame Chiang alone in her car, they took her back to the office—"for her own protection."

Du tried to pretend that he had not kidnapped Madame Chiang, but everyone knew that he had. Chiang paid a large sum of money to the Green Gang, and Madame Chiang learned to be more careful about upsetting Big-Eared Du. But it wasn't long before the Chiangs would put Shanghai behind them. In early January 1928, the couple headed north to the city of Nanking, which was now under Nationalist control. This would be the new capital of the Republic of China. ✍

至聖孔子

兗州府曲阜縣人

5 THE NEW LIFE MOVEMENT

❧❀❧

In Nanking, the Chiangs lived in grand style. Chiang was given the title generalissimo to honor his role as a military commander. As Nationalist leaders, he and his wife ate sumptuous banquets, bought expensive clothes, food, and cigarettes from other countries, and traveled in limousines.

But in the 1930s, most Chinese people were living in terrible conditions. The country did not have a system for health care, and deadly diseases spread quickly throughout the countryside. The nation did not have a good railroad or other transportation system, and people in many parts of the country starved because of a lack of food. Meanwhile, the Communist rebels were telling the Chinese peasants that under communism, they would have a better life

The teachings of fifth-century B.C. Chinese philosopher Confucius formed the basis for the New Life Movement of the 1930s.

The term generalissimo means "supreme commander" or "commander in chief" in Italian, although no Italians have ever used the title. Generalissimo Chiang Kai-shek was awarded his title in 1932 in honor of his achievements as a military leader. Today, the term is used most often in English to describe a ruler who has gained his position by a military overthrow.

and share in the country's wealth.

The Chiangs wanted China to become a powerful country that could hold its own among the mighty nations of the world, such as the Soviet Union and the United States. They wanted to rule over a prosperous and united China. But they knew they had to convince Chinese peasants that they would be better off under Nationalist rule than under communism.

The Nationalists and the Communists both believed in a strong government that would control the country's property and factories. But the Chiangs knew that Chinese people did not necessarily want to live in a modern world. For almost 2,000 years, the Chinese had lived by the teachings of Confucius, a philosopher from the fifth century B.C. Confucius had taught four principles: *Li*, behaving well; *Yi*, doing what is right instead of what helps you most; *Lian*, honesty; and *Qi*, integrity and honor. The Chiangs knew that they could build on these Chinese values to gain support for the Nationalists.

Generalissimo Chiang thought that many of the problems in China were due to people's laziness and sloppiness. He did not approve of Chinese people dressing sloppily, smoking in the streets, or otherwise behaving badly. He felt that a countrywide plan of orderliness would give new discipline to the Chinese people, and thus help them escape from poverty and sickness.

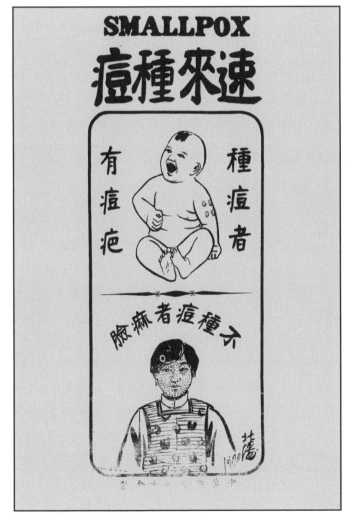

Smallpox was one of the many diseases that plagued China in the 1930s.

The philosopher Confucius (c. 551–479 B.C.) was one of the most famous people in ancient China. His teachings about the government, people's behavior, and the rules that should be followed to make a successful life continue to influence people today. Although Chiang Kai-shek often said that he based his governing style on Confucius, in fact, the ancient philosopher would not have agreed with the government oppression—ruling by fear and harsh discipline—practiced by the Nationalists.

Soon the Chiangs announced the start of China's New Life Movement. This movement had at its core a set of rules aimed at increasing discipline among the Chinese. It was based on the four principles of Confucius. Madame Chiang explained that *Li* would show outsiders the best native qualities of the Chinese, and *Yi* would keep people from "hold[ing] wealth and enjoy[ing] it wastefully while our fellow countrymen may be on the verge of starvation or suffering from sickness or other evils." *Lian* would make government officials recognize the rights of the people, while *Qi* would mean that "no one would become shameless or stoop to anything mean or underhand."

A long list of New Life Movement rules was published and posted in many cities and villages around China. A traditional Chinese lantern parade was held in one city, with signs printed with slogans like "Be prompt," "Don't spit," "Be neat," or more specific instructions like "Kill flies and rats: They breed disease," and "Avoid wine, women and gambling." The New Life rules required people to live simply, to waste no money, to behave well, and to buy Chinese products.

As far as living simply, the Chinese people were told to replace fancy wedding ceremonies—like the one held by the Chiangs in 1927—with simple at-home ceremonies. Since most people in China could not afford large wedding ceremonies anyway, the rules

The New Life Movement supported smaller marriage ceremonies performed in the home.

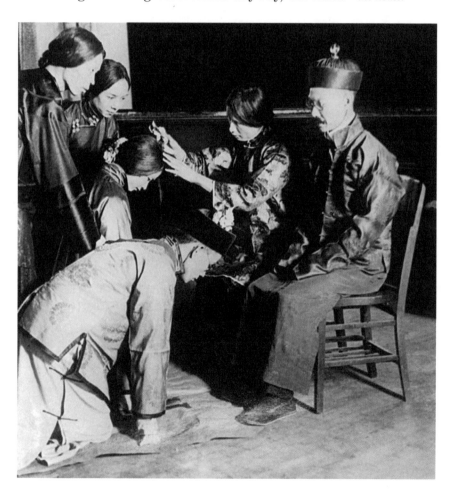

did not affect them. And many wealthy people simply ignored the rules. For instance, one rule called for alcohol and cigarettes to be forbidden. But inside the private homes of wealthy Chinese—especially the Nationalist leaders—alcohol and cigarettes remained common. Even Madame Chiang continued to order her cigarettes from abroad, breaking both the rule against smoking and the rule against buying things made in other countries. To discourage wasting money and food, there were limits in restaurants about how many dishes one table could order. But restaurants found a way to get around this by serving many dishes on the same platter. They also served alcohol in traditional Chinese teapots.

During this time, when American and European fashions were becoming popular among Chinese city residents, many specific rules applied to how women should dress. In some places, women's skirts had to be at least ankle-length, the distance between the collar and the cheek could be no more than an inch and a half (4 centimeters), sleeves had to reach at least the elbow, slits on skirts could not be above the knees, and tight dresses were not allowed. Also, women were ordered to comb their hair back and not let it fall beneath their necks, and were forbidden from curling it. Many women had recently begun to work in government offices, where they were required to wear short blue jackets, black skirts,

According to New Life rules, Chinese women were to wear long, loose dresses with high collars.

black stockings, and black shoes. Across the country, "citizen detectives" were encouraged to report rule violations. In one town, a citizen dumped acid on a woman he thought was dressed inappropriately.

While many of the New Life rules seemed needlessly strict, some were quite practical. One rule encouraged vaccinating children against common diseases. Another forbade urinating in the street, which had been quite common in many towns. These rules helped improve health across the country. But for the most part, the New Life Movement was either out of touch with Chinese lives—as with the rules forbidding overeating to people who could barely afford to feed their families one meal of rice per day—or the rules were ignored—as wealthy Chinese ignored the ones about going to bed early and avoiding alcohol. In fact, the vast majority of Chinese people could not read and never learned of the New Life Movement.

The difference between the realities of Chinese life and the New Life rules showed how out of touch the Chiangs were becoming. The New Life Movement focused on changing aspects of behavior such as dress and discipline. It did little to solve the real problems of a nation where most of the people were suffering from starvation or disease.

While more and more Chinese were doing without, the Chiangs were becoming wealthier and more powerful. The Chiangs divided their time between their Nanking headquarters and their house in the Lushan Mountains above the Yangtze River. Madame Chiang imported many items from Europe to furnish this mountain retreat. The Chiangs spent summers there, surrounded by bodyguards and servants. The generalissimo, his secretary, and his private doctor had a

Map legend:

- ⊛ Capital of Republic of China, 1928–1949
- ⊛ Capital of Republic of China, 1949–present
- ⊛ Capital of People's Republic of China, 1949–present

Map shows boundaries of 1949.

Lake Baikal

SOVIET UNION

N / W E / S

0   450 miles
0   450 kilometers

MONGOLIA

NORTH KOREA

PAKISTAN

Beijing ⊛

SOUTH KOREA

C H I N A
(Republic of China, 1912–1949;
People's Republic of China, 1949–present)

JAPAN

Xi'an •

Nanking ⊛ • Shanghai

TIBET

Hankou • *Whangpoo River*

River

Lushan Mountains • Fenghua

NEPAL BHUTAN

Chungking

I N D I A

PAKISTAN

Taoyuan ⊛ Taipei

Taiwan

EUROPE

A S I A

China

BURMA

French Indochina

Hainan

AUSTRALIA

THAILAND

PHILIPPINES

South China Sea

Yangtze

wing of the first floor. Madame Chiang had her own bedroom, furnished with a double bed from England, leather armchairs, a lounge chair, and a wooden desk. The bathroom had an imported green bathtub and fixtures. Madame Chiang spent her days playing her upright piano, painting landscapes, and reading from her collection of English-language books. ✐

Madame Chiang spent much of her life in China in cities on or near the coast.

53 ᐧᑯᑐ

6 SAVING THE GENERALISSIMO

༺~~~༻

While the New Life Movement may have had little impact on the lives of most Chinese citizens, the Nationalist government did begin some projects that would improve lives. A system of roads connecting China's spread-out cities and towns was begun in the 1930s. The government also built up factories and industries, especially in coastal cities like Shanghai. And the Nationalists announced that their goal was to provide free education for every Chinese citizen. In fact, from 1926 to 1935, the number of high schools tripled, but that still meant that only a small percentage of Chinese people were being educated. Wealthy city residents continued to send their children to school abroad, just as the Soongs had sent their children to the United States. And Chinese

Generalissimo Chiang (right) met with Chang Hsueh-liang, the "Young Marshal," when the two were still allies.

companies rewarded overseas education. At one company, American college graduates earned four times as much as Chinese college graduates, and the American graduates were also rewarded with fancier desks and crystal inkstands for their pens.

One of the overall goals of the Nationalists was to modernize the nation of China. Madame Chiang, in particular, admired many aspects of modern American and European life. She had long been fascinated with airplanes, and in 1936 she became secretary general of the Chinese Commission on Aeronautical Affairs. Although she actually suffered from airsickness, she did not let that interfere with her love of airplanes. She believed that in order to become a true world power, China would need to build up a powerful air force. She later said, "Of all of the inventions that have helped to unify China, perhaps the airplane is the most outstanding."

Madame Chiang was the ideal face for promoting air power throughout China. She was, of course, more familiar with the world outside of China than her husband was. She understood the power of modern technology. But she also understood diplomacy and the idea that sometimes befriending the enemy is the best way to win a war. Madame Chiang was skilled at getting people to talk to her, listen to her, and admire her. As her husband increased his power and gained more enemies within China, Madame Chiang

Madame Chiang was popular with China's troops.

soon found the chance to use her diplomatic skills to rescue him.

In December 1936, Generalissimo Chiang was resting at a mountain hot spring resort near Xi'an in northern China. As he did every morning of his life, Chiang woke early and did his morning exercises. On December 12, he was exercising in his nightshirt when he heard shouting and gunshots outside. He recognized that he was under attack and climbed out the back window, leaving his uniform, his shoes, and his false

Generalissimo Chiang was attacked while at Xi'an's Huaqing Hot Springs.

teeth in the room. Escaping up the snow-covered hill behind the building, he tripped, hurting his knee and his back. He could barely walk any farther when he found shelter inside a cave behind a large rock.

For hours, the leader of China huddled, freezing cold and barely dressed, inside the cave. Finally, he decided he could not take it any longer. When he heard voices outside his cave, he crawled out and surrendered. With bloody feet and skin blue with cold, Chiang asked his captors for a horse to carry him down the hill. The commander of the attack addressed Chiang respectfully by his formal title and said they had no horse but that he himself would carry Chiang down the hill. The commander knelt, and after a moment's hesitation, Chiang climbed on his back. At the bottom of the hill, Chiang was put into a waiting car.

After being taken to a military headquarters, Chiang learned that he had been kidnapped under orders from Chang Hsueh-liang. Also known as the Young Marshal, Chang was a powerful warlord and former ally of Chiang's. He believed the Nationalist government should stop fighting China's Communists and instead concentrate on resisting Japan. Since the mid-1930s, Japan had been attacking China and taking over Chinese land. Chang wanted the Nationalists and the Communists to work together to stop the Japanese. He told Chiang he would free him on the condition that he join the Communists in a fight against Japan. But Chiang refused to cooperate with his kidnappers. "If you want to kill me, kill me now," he said.

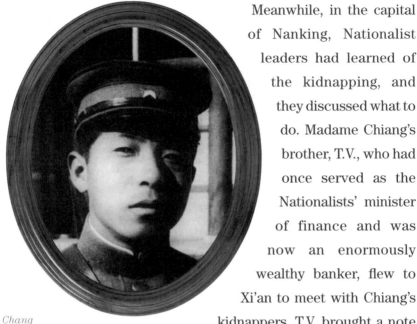

Chang Hsueh-liang, the "Young Marshal" (1901–2001)

Meanwhile, in the capital of Nanking, Nationalist leaders had learned of the kidnapping, and they discussed what to do. Madame Chiang's brother, T.V., who had once served as the Nationalists' minister of finance and was now an enormously wealthy banker, flew to Xi'an to meet with Chiang's kidnappers. T.V. brought a note from Madame Chiang to her husband, in which she told him that if her brother did not return within three days, "I will come to live and die with you." T.V. tried to organize Chiang's release, but the generalissimo refused to give in to any of the kidnappers' demands for his freedom. He would not promise to give up any of his power to unite with the Communists. After three days, T.V. flew back to Nanking alone.

Madame Chiang decided that she herself needed to go to Xi'an to help win her husband's freedom. She traveled with her Australian adviser, William Donald, her husband's spare set of false teeth, and her pistol. She and Donald decided that they would try to talk nicely with the kidnappers and win Chiang's freedom through friendliness. She stepped off the plane in Xi'an in a long, black coat with a fur collar, looking as impressive as ever. She immediately demanded to meet with her husband and was taken down a long hallway past guards with machine guns. Then she was led into a room where she saw her husband "lying there injured and helpless, a shadow of his former self."

Madame Chiang was furious at how her husband was being treated,

Nanking lies on the Yangtze River, about 200 miles (320 kilometers) from the East China Sea. The city served as China's capital during several historical periods. Though Beijing became China's capital in 1949, Nanking remains a provincial capital and is an important center of industry, transportation, government, and culture in east-central China.

but she remained friendly in her meetings with the kidnappers. Chang and the other kidnappers had by now agreed that if the Communists were satisfied, they would free Chiang. But the Communists said they wanted a written pledge from Chiang that he would cooperate with them. Chiang refused to write such a pledge. But Madame Chiang met with Communist leaders and hinted that her husband would end his war with the Communists. "Internal problems should be solved by political means, and not by military force," she said. This hardly sounded truthful coming from the wife of the man who had used military force to rule China, but the Communists agreed that they would accept this as Generalissimo Chiang's word. On December 25, 1936, he was released. Madame Chiang's skills at diplomacy had probably saved his life—and perhaps the Chinese Nationalist government as well.

By the end of the 1930s, China was involved in full-scale war with the Japanese, often called the Second Sino-Japanese War (1937–1945). Although there was an official peace agreement between the Nationalists and the Communists, they never actually fought together against the Japanese. In fact, because of Chiang's anti-communist policies, he received much help from Nazi Germany, which was also anti-communist and sent the Nationalists many weapons. In addition, many Nationalist leaders, including Chiang's son, Chiang Ching-kuo, were trained in the German army.

Madame Chiang took a leading role in the war effort. She continued to push the development of the air force, especially the purchase of airplanes from the United States.

China and Japan clashed previously in the Sino-Japanese War of 1894–1895. This conflict was fought over control of Korea, in which both countries had political and economic interests. Japan was victorious, and Korea was ultimately declared an independent nation. China was forced to pay Japan $150 million and give up the island of Taiwan. The island was eventually claimed by the Nationalists in 1945.

She also visited wounded soldiers in the hospital and organized a program in which women sewed 2 million winter uniforms for the Chinese troops.

While the war between Japan and China raged, much of the rest of the world was involved in

In her program to sew winter uniforms for Chinese soldiers, Madame Chiang led by example.

World War II. In this war, the Allied forces (mainly the United States, Britain, France, and the Soviet Union) were fighting the Germans and the Japanese. The United States now needed the help of China in its war against Japan. Throughout the 1930s, Generalissimo and Madame Chiang had become known in the United States as democratic crusaders against communism. This was due in part to Madame Chiang's engaging

An elderly woman and young boy sat amid the rubble after a Japanese bombing attack on Chungking, China.

personality and knowledge of the English language and American customs. It was also largely the result of efforts by Henry Luce, the powerful American publisher of *Time* magazine.

Henry Luce's parents had been missionaries in China, and Luce was committed to Christianizing and Americanizing China. He named the Chiangs "Man and Woman of the Year" in 1937 and put them on the cover of *Time*. In 1941, he came to Nanking as a guest of the Chiangs. Madame Chiang carefully organized his 10-day visit so that he would see the Nationalist government in the best possible light. At the end of his visit, Luce wrote that Generalissimo Chiang was the greatest ruler China had seen for 250 years. He committed himself to helping the Nationalist cause and put Chiang on the cover of *Time* half a dozen times. 🐦

In 1938, Madame Chiang published a collection of her English-language speeches and writings. The book, titled Madame Chiang's Messages in War and Peace, was printed on special imported paper and bound in blue silk. Ten thousand copies were printed and distributed internationally.

Chapter

7 TAKING THE STATES BY STORM

❧❦❧

Madame Chiang was becoming more and more popular with the Chinese people. She traveled throughout the country, with her husband and on her own, working to unify China. She was popular inside China because of her vast knowledge of Chinese languages, literature, and traditions. But foreigners were perhaps her greatest admirers. During World War II, many British and American diplomats came to China. As an English speaker, Madame Chiang was able to show and tell them just what she wanted them to see and hear. She told foreign visitors that everything was going well, even when it was not.

To the United States, it was important that China win its war against Japan; this would help the United States defeat Japan in World War II. To help achieve

Madame Chiang met with first lady Eleanor Roosevelt during her triumphant 1943 visit to the United States.

this goal, the United States sent millions of dollars for the Chinese army in the 1930s and 1940s. To Madame Chiang, it was important that Americans admired the Nationalists and herself personally. She wanted China to be a superpower, equal to the United States. And she wanted the Chiangs to be world leaders.

American General Joseph Stilwell was one of the many foreign diplomats who admired the capability and power of Madame Chiang. Their friendship began when Stilwell was sent to China in 1942. As chief of staff to the generalissimo, Stilwell was supposed to help the Chinese army defeat the Japanese. But he and the generalissimo did not get along. Stilwell suspected that the Nationalists, and the Chiangs personally, were stealing some of the aid money sent by the United States. He also thought the Nationalists did not have a good plan to defeat the Japanese. But Stilwell admired Madame Chiang and the role she played in the war effort. He even suggested, only half-jokingly, that she be named China's minister of defense. In his diary, he described the woman he called Madame Empress:

> *Quick, intelligent. Wants to get things done. Wishes she was a man. Doesn't think deeply, but catches on in a hurry. Very frank and open. ... A clever, brainy woman. ... Direct, forceful, energetic, loves*

*power, eats up publicity and flattery,
pretty weak on her history. No concession
to the Western viewpoint in all China's foreign relations. The Chinese were always
right; the foreigners were always wrong.*

Indeed, Madame Chiang concentrated most of her efforts on showing the world that the Chinese were always right. She wrote articles to be published in foreign newspapers and magazines. Her photograph appeared throughout the world, and she became known as the face of modern China. She worked

Though he had a difficult relationship with the generalissimo, General Stilwell (right) got along well with Madame Chiang.

endlessly, and her efforts took a toll on her health. By 1942, she was suffering from exhaustion, a bad back, dental problems, skin rashes, and breathing trouble. Many of her health problems were caused by her constant smoking, but she was too busy to change her lifestyle.

In late 1942, 44-year-old Madame Chiang made a trip to the United States. The main purpose of the trip was to seek medical help. In addition to her other illnesses, the generalissimo thought his wife might have stomach cancer. He wanted her

Chinese-Americans across the United States were excited about Madame Chiang's visit.

to get tests done in the United States that were not available in China. She flew to New York with two nurses and her niece. At the airport, she was met by a close aide to President Roosevelt and taken directly to the hospital.

At the New York hospital, Madame Chiang set the tone for her United States visit. She had an entire floor reserved for her, and she demanded constant attention by doctors. But despite her illnesses, she wanted to talk politics with important visitors whenever possible. First lady Eleanor Roosevelt visited her three times during her month-long hospital stay. Madame Chiang wanted to talk about the war and the importance of the United States helping China. But Roosevelt remembered that Madame Chiang was in great pain. She wrote:

> *She seemed to me quite nervous and suffering a great deal; she could hardly bear to have anything touch any part of her body. Madame Chiang seemed so petite and delicate ... that I had a desire to help her and take care of her as I would my own daughter.*

In fact, Roosevelt had a special reason for wanting to care for Madame Chiang: When the Roosevelts' son James, a Marine, had visited China after undergoing a stomach operation, Madame Chiang had made sure that he was well cared for. To Madame Chiang, a good relationship with the U.S. president and his wife was essential in winning China respect as a superpower.

When Madame Chiang was released from the hospital, she spent a few weeks at the Roosevelts' home in New York state. She soon decided that she was feeling well enough to tour the United States, speaking to audiences about the importance of U.S. support for China and raising money for the Nationalist cause. Henry Luce, who had already helped make her popular in the United States, offered to pay expenses for her trip.

Madame Chiang began her tour with a February 1943 visit to the White House. Although the Roosevelts wanted to be welcoming to the first lady of China, they were sometimes annoyed by her behavior. She had brought her own supply of silk sheets, and she demanded that they be changed every day—and twice a day if she took a nap. She also flirted with almost all the men she came in contact with. But the Roosevelts also understood that their visitor was "hard as steel." At one White House dinner, the president asked Madame Chiang how striking workers were dealt with in China. She drew her long, red-painted nail across her throat, saying that they would be killed immediately.

For the most part, however, Madame Chiang charmed the Americans she met. During her stay at the White House, she was invited to address Congress, where she received a standing ovation. Eleanor Roosevelt and Vice President Henry Wallace held a banquet in her honor, at which everyone was impressed by Madame Chiang's charm, her fashionable appearance, and her ability to speak intelligently about politics.

Early in March 1943, Madame Chiang returned to New York, where she was greeted by the mayor, Fiorello LaGuardia. "I wish to tell you that although we have suffered we have been able to carry on

Madame Chiang spoke to a huge crowd in New York City in 1943.

because we knew the American people were with us," she told LaGuardia.

While in New York, Madame Chiang stayed at the Waldorf-Astoria, one of the city's finest hotels. She had an entire floor to herself, and bodyguards cleared the hallways and elevators when she came or went. On March 2, she spoke to a crowd of nearly 20,000 people in New York's Madison Square Garden. Her voice was pumped out on loudspeakers and broadcast on the radio to millions of Americans. "All nations, great and small, must have equal opportunity to develop," she told the crowd. "Those who are stronger and more advanced should consider their strength as a trust to be used to help the weaker nations to fit themselves for full self-government." Praise for the great strength of the United States was exactly what patriotic Americans wanted to hear during the war. Many donated money to the Nationalist efforts in China. An article in *The New York Times* noted, "Whatever she desired, had it been in the people's power, would have been granted."

The rest of Madame Chiang's American tour was just as successful. She addressed huge crowds in Boston, Chicago, and Los Angeles. She showed a kind, intelligent, and modern face of China to the United States. She visited Wellesley College, where she had graduated 26 years earlier. She walked across the Wellesley campus in slacks, which were not acceptable dress for Wellesley women. But the college president said, "Anyone who can look as smart as Madame Chiang in slacks may wear them." Everywhere she went, Madame Chiang spoke about the suffering in China and the need for the United States to help China win its war against Japan. She collected millions of dollars for her United China Relief Fund.

In Hollywood, California, Madame Chiang met with movie stars, including Henry Fonda, Ingrid

Madame Chiang greeted actress Marlene Dietrich at a reception during her 1943 U.S. tour.

Bergman, Ginger Rogers, Shirley Temple, and Rita Hayworth. More than 30,000 people attended a fundraising event at the Hollywood Bowl, where the Los Angeles Philharmonic played "The Madame Chiang Kai-shek March." Henry Luce put Madame Chiang on the cover of *Time* again. She had become one of the

In 1943, Madame Chiang was featured on the cover of Time *magazine.*

most famous and recognized faces in the United States.

Overall, Madame Chiang excelled at gaining sympathy for the Chinese among Americans and at showing the similarities between the two countries. Some U.S. government officials even worried about her effect on American citizens. They worried that she would convince Americans that it was more important to support the Chinese against the Japanese than it was to win the war in Europe against Germany. But by the end of her visit, President Roosevelt had agreed to send several hundred new airplanes for the Chinese air force. Since she had long been certain of the necessity of a powerful air force, the promise of planes was one more victory for Madame Chiang.

In 1942 and 1943, Madame Chiang was considered by some to be the most powerful woman in the world. During that period of World War II, the Allied powers—the United States, Russia, and Great Britain—felt they needed China to help defeat the Japanese. As the international face of the Nationalists, and one of the few English speakers, Madame Chiang was involved in most communications between the United States and China. The U.S. State Department even had a code name for her: Snow White.

8 HARDSHIP IN CHINA

Chapter

❦❧

While Madame Chiang was receiving standing ovations in the United States, the living conditions of the Chinese people were getting worse. Floods caused crop failures in some parts of the country, while a lack of rain dried out other parts. Diseases were spreading quickly throughout the country, and a plague of locusts swarmed over central China. Across the country, Chinese people were dying of starvation or disease. Instead of focusing on the famine, the Nationalists continued to use all their resources to support the army troops in their fight against the Japanese. As one general explained, "If the people die, the land will still be Chinese. But if the soldiers starve, the Japanese will take the land."

Madame Chiang, however, was so popular—

To Madame Chiang and other Chinese, the surrender of the Japanese to the Allied forces in World War II was a victory for China as well.

> One of the Nationalist government's responses to China's failing economy was to print more and more paper money, called yuan. This oversupply of currency made the money worthless. Soon several million yuan equaled one U.S. dollar. Millions of panicked citizens tried to pull their savings out of banks, only to find that the banks didn't have the money to give them.

and powerful—that she was able to influence what most of the world heard about conditions in China. She wanted the world to know that the Chinese were suffering during the war, but she did not want anyone to know that the Nationalist government was ignoring the suffering of the Chinese people while it continued its fight against Japan. When a *Time* reporter traveled around China and wrote a harsh story about the corruption of the Nationalist government, including details of stolen aid money and the way the government ignored starving citizens, Madame Chiang asked Henry Luce to fire the reporter. Luce would not fire the reporter, but he only allowed a small part of the story to get printed in *Time*. The printed story contained no mention of government corruption.

Madame Chiang's American trip was a great success, but her reputation was hurt almost as soon as she began her return trip to China. Chiang and her niece left the United States together in early July 1943. They were carrying such a large amount of luxury items that they had to pack several crates and send some on another aircraft. When they landed in India for a layover, one of the crates was dropped and fell open. The American soldiers who were helping unload the baggage got a glimpse of the contents. Inside the broken crate were fancy groceries, cigarettes, cosmetics, and other luxury items. The American soldiers, who had been living without such luxuries for years and knew about the suffering in China, were angry that the first lady of China was wasting money on these items.

In China, famine and disease continued to spread. Thousands of people were dying every day. Although

During the Sino-Japanese War, people throughout China suffered from starvation and disease.

the Nationalists had intentions of improving roads, schools, and health care, the long war with Japan had taken all of their resources. Instead of being able to help the citizens, the Nationalists cracked down on anyone who opposed them. They accused anyone who criticized them of being a Communist, for which the punishment was execution. Back at home, Madame Chiang traveled around China, building support for the Nationalist cause. But she probably did not see the true suffering of the Chinese people, since each village she visited was scrubbed up and decorated for her arrival.

In late 1943, the Chiangs achieved some of the world respect they craved when China was asked to join with the United States, Great Britain, and the Soviet Union at a meeting of the Big Four Allied powers. Leaders from these four nations met in Cairo, Egypt, and Madame Chiang accompanied her husband. She was present at the first meeting between the world leaders, wearing a black satin dress with bright yellow flowers, a fitted black jacket, a black veil over her face, and large black bows at the back of her head. Since the generalissimo spoke no English, she took the opportunity to act as translator whenever she could. She often interrupted the official translator to make sure her own view was getting across. Unfortunately for the Chiangs, the result of the talks was that the United States would concentrate

more efforts on the fighting in Europe and less on the fight with China against the Japanese. This led to less American aid to China and freed the U.S. government to look more closely at the Nationalist government. In turn, it revealed Chiang's treatment of the Chinese people and improper handling of aid money.

In Cairo, Madame Chiang met with U.S. President Roosevelt (center left) and British Prime Minister Winston Churchill (center right).

The unhappy results of the Cairo meeting, together with her hectic schedule, worsened Madame Chiang's health problems. By late 1944, she had developed a painful skin rash and suffered from exhaustion. She made another trip abroad to rest and seek medical treatment. Traveling with her sister Ailing, she first visited Brazil. While Madame Chiang rested, Ailing met with the Brazilian ruler to discuss hiding some of the family fortune in Brazil, where it would be safer than in China. Next, the sisters traveled to New York, where Madame Chiang entered a hospital for a month of treatment. After leaving the hospital, she hoped to repeat her successful earlier American tour. By now, however, many Americans had heard rumors about the corruption of the Chinese Nationalists and were not as quickly impressed by Madame Chiang as they had been just 18 months earlier.

However, thanks to British and American efforts,

The three Soong sisters, (from left) Meiling, Ailing, and Qingling, all became very powerful women in China.

the country was winning its war against Japan. In 1945, Japan was finally defeated, and the Chinese Nationalists and Communists returned to fighting each other. Both groups were determined to rule a united China. Now that World War II was over, the United States turned its attention to fighting communism as well. The U.S. government continued to send advisers, weapons, and large sums of money to help the Nationalists.

It was becoming more and more obvious, however, that the Nationalists were mishandling U.S. aid. Specifically, the Chiang and Soong families were stealing large sums of aid money. Madame Chiang's brother, T.V., was China's foreign minister. Almost all of the American aid money was sent to China through him, and he often skimmed large amounts of this money and placed it in his own personal bank account. He began investing the money by buying real estate and other goods in South America, where it was difficult for the U.S. government to track his dealings. When the United Nations Relief and Rehabilitation Association

With the Nationalists and the Communists again at odds, conditions in China became even more desperate. At times, even soldiers were without food. Foreign newspaper reporters wrote that it was not uncommon to find Nationalist soldiers begging for food. Although the soldiers were supposed to be paid for their service, they often did not receive their wages, and even if they did, the money was often not worth anything.

(UNRRA) sent supplies to help the Chinese people, government officials stole the goods and sold them on the illegal black market. One American visitor to central China reported that soldiers were stealing supplies intended for an orphanage, and the children there were dying without food and medicine. After an American doctor tried to make sure a train full of supplies reached starving people in a Communist area of northern China, Nationalist soldiers diverted the car to a remote location and left him to die of cold and hunger.

In November 1948, Madame Chiang returned to the United States to plead for more aid. She hoped to repeat her successful fund raising of five years earlier. "I can ask the American people for nothing more," she said. "It is either in your hearts to love us, or your hearts have been turned from us." But President Harry Truman was fed up with the wastefulness and corruption of the Nationalists. He believed that they were incapable of winning the civil war with the Chinese Communists, and he did not want to waste any more U.S. money on the effort. "They're thieves, every ... one of

During World War II, the U.S. government sent more than $3 billion in aid money to the Nationalists. In 1948, the U.S. Congress approved another $1 billion to help the fight against the Chinese Communists. But the vast amounts of money seemed to do little good. Much of the money was stolen by the Chiangs or the Soongs, and in any event, the problems in China were too severe by that time to be solved by extra money.

them," Truman later said of the Nationalist leaders.

Madame Chiang was unable to convince the United States to send more aid to China. She never returned to the Chinese mainland.

In January 1949, the generalissimo resigned as president of Nationalist China. By the end of that year, the Chinese Communist army gained control over the last of China's cities, and Chiang was forced to flee. He took a plane to the Chinese island of Taiwan, 100 miles (160 km) from the mainland. On December 8, 1949, he declared Taipei, Taiwan, the temporary capital of the Republic of China. He was elected president, and Madame Chiang joined her husband in Taiwan. 🐉

U.S. President Harry Truman met with Madame Chiang during her 1948 trip to the United States.

9 IN EXILE

⤞⋄⤝

Nearly 2 million loyal Nationalists followed the Chiangs to Taiwan. The Chiangs also brought the national art collection. They kept the valuable paintings, ceramics, and other items in crates in their new home in Taipei. They planned to take them back to China as soon as they regained control over the mainland. They believed that they would one day return to rule over the entire Republic of China.

Meanwhile, the Chinese Communists established the People's Republic of China on the mainland and did not recognize the Republic of China, based in Taiwan and led by Chiang. The Communist leader Mao Tse-tung ruled the People's Republic and planned to invade Taiwan. But the United States sent U.S. Navy forces to guard the small island. Although

The Chiangs were joined in Taiwan by Chiang Ching-kuo (right), General Chiang's son from his first marriage.

Mao Tse-tung
(1893–1976)

many people in the U.S. government did not agree with all of Chiang's ideas, they agreed that they needed to support his government in the growing fight against communism. For the rest of the 1950s, the U.S. Navy protected Taiwan. In 1954, Chiang Kai-shek was reelected president of the Republic of China, as his Taiwan government continued to call itself. Later that year, Taiwan and the United States signed a treaty, with the United States agreeing to take action against the Chinese mainland if the Communists attacked Taiwan.

Generalissimo and Madame Chiang ruled over the Taiwanese government for 26 years. During those years of the Cold War, the United States gave military protection to Taiwan and recognized the government there as the only government of China. Taiwan also represented China in the world governing body, the United Nations. Throughout the 1950s, Madame Chiang made several trips to the United States to argue against the communist People's Republic of China being given a U.N. seat. Meanwhile, her husband governed Taiwan much as he had ruled mainland China—as a dictator. But he also ended much of the corruption that marked the Nationalists in China and paved the way for Taiwan to become the wealthy nation that it is today.

Madame Chiang continued to play a prominent international role. She was the honorary chair of the American Bureau for Medical Aid to China, a patron of the International Red Cross Committee, honorary chair of the British United Aid to China Fund, and first honorary member of the Bill of Rights Commemorative Society. Through the late 1960s, she was almost always included on lists of the 10 most admired women by Americans. She began to spend more and more time in the United States and eventually purchased a home in Lattingtown, on New York's Long Island. She also devoted more of her time to painting, a hobby she had had little time for since the early days of her marriage, when the Chiangs spent their summers in China's Lushan Mountains.

Taiwan is an island about 100 miles (160 km) from the southeastern coast of China, slightly smaller than the combined states of Delaware and Maryland. The island has a tropical climate and is about two-thirds covered by mountains. Historically, Taiwan has been a part of China, but from 1895 through the end of World War II, it was controlled by the Japanese. Since the Chinese Nationalists established their "government in exile" on the island in 1949, it has developed into one of the wealthiest Asian nations.

In 1975, Chiang Kai-shek had a heart attack and suffered for several months with pneumonia. On

April 5 of that year, he died. His son Chiang Ching-kuo from his first marriage took over as Taiwan's president. The generalissimo's body was kept in a temporary mausoleum in Taoyuan, Taiwan. His family hoped that he could eventually be buried at his birth-place in Fenghua in eastern China, following the Chinese custom of returning to the place of one's birth in death.

After her husband's death, Madame Chiang moved permanently to New York, where by now many of her relatives had also moved. In 1976, she was diagnosed with breast cancer and received treatment in New York. But she continued to follow politics in Taiwan, and when her stepson died in 1988, she returned to the island to try to join the new government. She was unable to gain enough support and soon returned to the United States. She moved to an apartment in Manhattan, where her black-suited bodyguards cleared out the elevator and lobby whenever she came or went, just as they had 45 years earlier when she had stayed at New York's Waldorf-Astoria hotel.

In 1995, Madame Chiang made a last appearance before Congress. In 1998, she celebrated her 100th birthday. That same year, near-riots erupted when she held an auction of 800 items from her Lattingtown, New York, estate. Police were called in to control the thousands of Chinese-Americans who wanted

to simply tour the home of the legendary woman who played such a large role in almost a century of Chinese history.

Although Madame Chiang had given up painting since moving from Taiwan, she displayed some of her paintings in San Francisco in 2000. Thousands of

Madame Chiang spent the early and final years of her life on the East Coast of the United States.

visitors toured the exhibition, titled "New Millennium Painting and Calligraphy by Madame Chiang Kai-shek and the Masters of Chinese Painting and Calligraphy." The exhibit included 10 never-before-seen works of Madame Chiang. But visitors were especially interested in one painting—*Lotus: A Gentleman Among Flowers*. Visitors gazed at the small gray ink sketch of a lotus among water lilies and carefully studied the hand-sketched inscription with a red seal at the top of the painting. The words were supposedly those of Generalissimo Chiang Kai-shek: "In a pure wind, I smell fragrance from afar. Sitting across from my wife, I forget the heat of summer."

In her final years, Madame Chiang lived alone in her apartment on Manhattan's Gracie Square. She was hard of hearing but said that she read the Bible and *The New York Times* daily. On October 23, 2003, at the age of 105, she died of old age. She was buried at Ferncliff Cemetery in Hartsdale, New York, although her long-term goal was to be buried alongside her husband in mainland China once political conditions made that possible.

Madame Chiang Kai-shek was a complicated woman, and she left a complicated legacy. Her supporters admire her as a force for international friendship and understanding, but others criticize her as one who sought power for its own sake rather than for the opportunities it provided to make the

Taiwan's Vice President Annette Lu paid her last respects to Madame Chiang in a memorial service in Taipei.

world a better place. What most everyone can agree upon, however, is the extent of her influence. In the United States, she was the model of what many Americans hoped China would become. Around the world, she was known as the face of modern China. Today, she is remembered as an influential leader, one of the most powerful and popular women of the 20th century. ❧

MADAME CHIANG KAI-SHEK'S LIFE

1898

Born Soong Meiling in Shanghai, China

1908

Travels to the United States to study near Macon, Georgia

1917

Graduates from Wellesley College near Boston, Massachusetts, and returns to China

1905

1901

Britain's Queen Victoria dies

1909

The National Association for the Advancement of Colored People (NAACP) is founded

1917

Vladimir Lenin and Leon Trotsky lead Bolsheviks in a rebellion against the czars in Russia during the October Revolution

WORLD EVENTS

1922

Meets Chiang Kai-shek at a dinner party hosted by her sister Ailing

1927

Marries Chiang Kai-shek in Shanghai; is kidnapped and briefly held by gangsters from the Green Gang

1928

Moves to Nanking, the Nationalist capital of the Republic of China

1925

1922

The tomb of Tutankhamen is discovered by British archaeologist Howard Carter

1926

Impressionist painters Claude Monet and Mary Cassat die

1928

Penicillin, the first antibiotic, is discovered by Scottish scientist Alexander Fleming

MADAME CHIANG KAI-SHEK'S LIFE

1936

Helps arrange husband's release after his kidnapping by rebel warlords

1937

With husband, named *Time* magazine's "Man and Woman of the Year"

1940

1933

Nazi leader Adolf Hitler is named chancellor of Germany

1936

African-American athlete Jesse Owens wins four gold medals at the Olympic Games in Berlin in the face of Nazi racial discrimination

1939

German troops invade Poland; Britain and France declare war on Germany; World War II (1939-1945) begins

WORLD EVENTS

1942

Returns to the United States to seek medical treatment for a bad back, skin rashes, and exhaustion

1943

Begins a highly successful tour of the United States; attends talks in Cairo, Egypt, with world leaders

1945

1941

Japanese bombers attack Pearl Harbor, Hawaii, on December 7, and the United States enters World War II

1945

The United States drops atomic bombs on Hiroshima and Nagasaki, Japan; World War II (1939–1945) ends

MADAME CHIANG KAI-SHEK'S LIFE

1948

Returns to the
United States
to plead for
more aid for the
Nationalists' war
against the Chinese
Communists

1949

Joins her husband in exile
on the island of Taiwan;
People's Republic of China
is formed

1950

1948

The modern
nation of Israel
is founded

1950

North Korea
invades South
Korea, which
begins the
Korean War

WORLD EVENTS

1975
Moves to New York City after the death of her husband

2000
Displays paintings in a San Francisco exhibition

2003
Dies in New York City on October 23 at the age of 105

2000

1974
Scientists find that chlorofluorocarbons—chemicals in coolants and propellants—are damaging Earth's ozone layer

2001
Terrorist attacks on the two World Trade Center Towers in New York City and on the Pentagon in Washington, D.C., leave thousands dead

2003
The United States and its allies invade Iraq

DATE OF BIRTH: Unknown month and
day (possibly March 5),
1898

BIRTHPLACE: Shanghai, China

FATHER: Charles (Charlie) Jones
Soong (1866–1918)

MOTHER: Ni Kwei-tseng
(1869–1931)

EDUCATION: Wellesley College,
Boston, Massachusetts

SPOUSE: Chiang Kai-shek
(1887–1975)

DATE OF MARRIAGE: December 1, 1927

DATE OF DEATH: October 23, 2003

PLACE OF BURIAL: Ferncliff Cemetery,
Hartsdale, New York,
pending relocation to
be buried alongside
her husband

FURTHER READING

Allan, Tony. *The Rise of Modern China*. Chicago: Heinemann Library, 2002.

Bo, Zhiyue. *The History of Modern China*. Philadelphia: Mason Crest Publishers, 2006.

Dolan, Sean. *Chiang Kai-shek*. New York: Chelsea House, 1988.

Rolka, Gail Meyer. *100 Women Who Shaped World History*. San Francisco: Bluewood Books, 1994.

Yen Mah, Adeline. *Chinese Cinderella: The True Story of an Unwanted Daughter*. New York: Dell Laurel-Leaf, 2001.

LOOK FOR MORE SIGNATURE LIVES BOOKS ABOUT THIS ERA:

Benazir Bhutto: *Pakistani Prime Minister and Activist*
ISBN 0-7565-1578-5

Fidel Castro: *Leader of Communist Cuba*
ISBN 0-7565-1580-7

Winston Churchill: *British Soldier, Writer, Statesman*
ISBN 0-7565-1582-3

Jane Goodall: *Legendary Primatologist*
ISBN 0-7565-1590-4

Adolf Hitler: *Dictator of Nazi Germany*
ISBN 0-7565-1589-0

Queen Noor: *American-born Queen of Jordan*
ISBN 0-7565-1595-5

Eva Perón: *First Lady of Argentina*
ISBN 0-7565-1585-8

Joseph Stalin: *Dictator of the Soviet Union*
ISBN 0-7565-1597-1

ON THE WEB

For more information on *Madame Chiang Kai-shek,* use FactHound.

1. Go to *www.facthound.com*
2. Type in this book ID: 0756518865
3. Click on the *Fetch It* button.

FactHound will find the best
Web sites for you.

HISTORIC SITES

Asian Art Museum
200 Larkin St.
San Francisco, CA 94102
415/581-3500
Galleries contain approximately 15,000
works of art spanning 6,000 years of
history and representing China and other
Asian cultures

San Diego Chinese Historical Museum
404 Third Ave.
San Diego, CA 92101
619/338-9888
Exhibits on Chinese culture and history, a
library of books on Chinese culture, and a
traditional Chinese garden

black market
the illegal sale or distribution of goods

communism
a system in which goods and property are owned by the government and shared in common

dictator
a ruler who takes complete control of a country, often unjustly

dynasty
a succession of rulers of the same line of descent

exile
living away from one's home country without the possibility of return

gangsters
members of a criminal gang

Industrial Revolution
a period from the middle 1700s to the 1800s of social and economic changes that took place during a transition from an agricultural and commercial society to an industrial society; the movement started in Great Britain and spread to Europe and the United States

mausoleum
a large building that houses a tomb or tombs

Nationalist
a political party, founded by Sun Yat-sen and led by Generalissimo Chiang Kai-shek, that struggled with the Communist Party for control of China

suffrage
the right to vote

warlord
a military commander exercising civil power by force, usually in a limited area

Chapter 1

Page 10, line 1: "Madame Chiang Kai-shek's Address to Senate." Scanned from the Congressional Record, 1943, pp. 1080–1081. *University of Michigan Library Documents Center.* 18 Feb. 1943. 11 April 2006. www.lib.umich.edu/govdocs/text/mchiang.htm

Page 12, line 7: Ibid.

Chapter 2

Page 18, line 8: Basil Miller. *Generalissimo and Madame Chiang Kai-shek: Christian Liberators of China.* Grand Rapids, Mich.: Zondervan, 1943, p. 22.

Page 21, line 5: Mur Wolf. "Madame Chiang Kai-shek: Wellesley Person of the Week." *Wellesley College.* 14 Aug. 2000. 11 April 2006. www.wellesley.edu/Anniversary/chiang.htmll

Chapter 3

Page 28, line 9: Jonathan Fenby. *Chiang Kai-shek: China's Generalissimo and the Nation He Lost.* New York: Carroll & Graf Publishers, 2003, p. 164.

Page 29, line 4: Ibid.

Page 29, line 9: Ibid., p. 165.

Page 29, line 11: Ibid.

Page 29, line 23: Ibid., p. 164.

Page 33, line 13: Ibid., p. 168.

Chapter 4

Page 35, line 6: Ibid., pp. 168–170.

Page 43, line 7: Ibid., p. 171.

Chapter 5

Page 48, line 11: Ibid., p. 246.

Page 48, line 19: Ibid.

Chapter 6

Page 56, line 16: "Mme. Chiang Kai-shek Dead At 106." *CBS News.* 24 Oct. 2003. 11 April 2006. www.cbsnews.com/stories/2003/10/24/world/main579764.shtml

Page 59, line 27: *Chiang Kai-shek: China's Generalissimo and the Nation He Lost,* p. 4.

Page 60, line 17: Ibid., p. 9.

Page 61, line 12: Ibid., p. 10.

Page 61, line 25: Ibid., p. 11.

Chapter 7

Page 68, line 24: Ibid., p. 387.

Page 71, line 17: Ibid., p. 393–394.

Page 72, line 22: Ibid., p. 394.

Page 73, line 10: *Generalissimo and Madame Chiang Kai-shek: Christian Liberators of China*, p. 174.

Page 74, line 10: Ibid.

Page 74, line 12: Ibid.

Page 74, line 20: Ibid., pp. 173–174.

Page 75, line 2: Mark Feeney. "Madame Chiang, Widow of Leader, at 106." *The Boston Globe*. 25 Oct. 2003. 18 April 2006. www.boston.com/news/education/higher/articles/2003/10/25/madame_chiang_widow_of_leader_at_106?mode=PF

Chapter 8

Page 79, line 12: *Chiang Kai-shek: China's Generalissimo and the Nation He Lost*, p. 398.

Page 86, line 16: "Soong Mei-ling Dies at 105." *The Korea Times*. 28 Oct. 2003. 18 April 2005. http://times.hankooki.com/plaza/ap_news.php?cur_date=20031028&page=5

Page 86, line 18: Ibid.

Page 86, line 28: *Chiang Kai-shek: China's Generalissimo and the Nation He Lost*, p. 480.

Chapter 9

Page 94, line 11: Ron Gluckman. "Madame Chiang Kai-shek and the Art of War." 11 April 2006. www.gluckman.com/ChiangKaiShek.htm

Publisher's Note: Some sources list Madame Chiang as having been born in 1897, making her 106 years old when she died in 2003. Based on all available information, the publisher prefers to cite 1898 as the year of her birth and 105 as her age at death. The Chinese usually consider everyone to be 1 year old at birth.

Chook, Shiu Heng. *Chiang Kai-shek Close-up: A Personal View.* Ed. Edward K. Chook. Oakland, Calif.: United California University Press, 1978.

Chu, Samuel C., ed. *Madame Chiang Kai-shek and Her China.* Norwalk, Conn.: EastBridge, 2004.

Faison, Seth. "Madame Chiang, 105, Chinese Leader's Widow, Dies." *New York Times.* 24 Oct. 2003.

Fenby, Jonathan. *Chiang Kai-shek: China's Generalissimo and the Nation He Lost.* New York: Carroll & Graf Publishers, 2003.

Feeney, Mark. "Madame Chiang, Widow of Leader, at 106." *The Boston Globe.* 25 Oct. 2003. 18 April 2006. www.boston.com/news/education/higher/articles/2003/10/25/madame_chiang_widow_of_leader_at_106?mode=PF

Furuya, Keiji. *Chiang Kai-shek: His Life and Times.* New York: St. John's University, 1981.

Gluckman, Ron. "Madame Chiang Kai-shek and the Art of War." 11 April 2006. www.gluckman.com/ChiangKaiShek.htm

Leong, Karen J. *China Mystique: Pearl S. Buck, Anna May Wong, Mayling Soong, and the Transformation of American Orientalism.* Berkeley, Calif.: University of California Press, 2005.

Miller, Basil. *Generalissimo and Madame Chiang Kai-shek: Christian Liberators of China.* Grand Rapids, Mich.: Zondervan, 1943.

Wolf, Mur. "Madame Chiang Kai-shek: Wellesley Person of the Week." *Wellesley College.* 14 Aug. 2000. 11 April 2006. www.wellesley.edu/Anniversary/chiang.html

"Mme. Chiang Kai-shek Dead At 106." *CBS News.* 24 Oct. 2003. 11 April 2006. www.cbsnews.com/stories/2003/10/24/world/main579764.shtml

"Madame Chiang Kai-shek's Address to Senate." Scanned from the Congressional Record, 1943, pp. 1080–1081. *University of Michigan Library Documents Center.* 18 Feb. 1943. 11 April 2006. www.lib.umich.edu/govdocs/text/mchiang.htm

"Soong Mei-ling Dies at 105." *The Korea Times.* 28 Oct. 2003. 18 April 2005. http://times.hankooki.com/plaza/ap_news.php?cur_date=20031028&page=5

Sandy Donovan has written several books for young readers about history, economics, government, and other topics. She has also worked as a newspaper reporter, a magazine editor, and a Web site developer. She has a bachelor's degree in journalism and a master's degree in public policy, and lives in Minneapolis, Minnesota, with her husband and two sons.

Image Credits